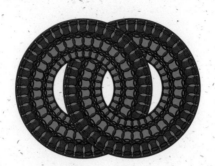

UNDERLIFE

UNDERLIFE

JANUARY GILL O'NEIL

January Gill O'Neil (signature)

CavanKerry ◈ Press LTD.

Library of Congress Cataloging-in-Publication Data

O'Neil, January Gill, 1969-
Underlife / January Gill O'Neil. – 1st ed.
p. cm.
ISBN-13: 978-1-933880-16-7 (alk. paper)
ISBN-10: 1-933880-16-3 (alk. paper)
I. Title.

PS3615.N435U53 2009
811'.6–dc22

2009037748
Cover art by Eric D. Stich © 2009,
Photography by Maureen Lederhos
Cover design by Peter Cusack
Book interior design by Denise Borel Billups

First Edition 2009
Printed in the United States of America

CavanKerry Press Ltd.
Fort Lee, New Jersey
www.cavankerrypress.org

CavanKerry Press is dedicated to springboarding the careers of previously unpublished poets by bringing to print two to three New Voices annually. Manuscripts are selected from open submission; CavanKerry Press does not conduct competitions.

CavanKerry is grateful for the support it receives from the New Jersey State Council on the Arts.

To my parents, for believing in me
To Alex and Ella, for loving me
To Phebus Etienne, for watching over me

CONTENTS

Dedication   vii

Foreword: Natasha Trethewey   xi

EARLY MEMORY

Nothing Fancy   3

Old Dog   4

Early Memory   5

Afro Puffs   6

Lightning Bugs   7

Service   8

Saturn's Child   9

Poem for My Father   10

She's Closest to Breaking   12

The Only Time I Ever Saw My Mother Drunk   13

Drinking   14

Permanent   15

Night Work   16

Self-Portrait   17

A TRUE STORY

How to Make a Crab Cake   21

In Praise of Okra   22

A True Story   24

The Young Girl   26

X's and O's   27

At the Subway   29

Drone   30

True Story #2: Missing   31

Poem About Nuts   33

Sex and Pizza   34

THE RIPE TIME

Morning Poem   39

Something I Needed   40

Sugar   41

Tuesday   42

Rough Country   43

The Ripe Time   44

The Fly   45

Not What You Expected   46

Always, There's Something   47

What the House Might Say   48

THE UNDERLIFE

Poem for My Infant Son   53

The Small Plans   54

Ella   55

Tangerines   57

The Kerning   58

What Mommy Wants   59

Discipline   60

Cow Logic   62

Back from Maternity Leave   63

The Editor Speaks   64

For Terence   65

Saying Yes   66

Contrition   67

Time Map   68

Take Care   69

Acknowledgments   71

Other Books in the New Voices Series   73

CavanKerry's Mission   74

FOREWORD

In her debut collection, *Underlife,* January O'Neil begins with a declaration of self rooted in home and family, and the ordinary tropes of childhood—fireflies, the schoolyard, and the daily rituals of our domestic lives. Yet this is no nostalgic portrait of bygone days. The smooth narrative surface of these poems gives way to gritty subjects— the underlife—where cruelties are commonplace, both given and received; where a child not only witnesses but also touches a parent's despair; where kinds of abuse fasten a yoke of longing and inheritance upon a daughter. As James Baldwin has written: *This is the only real concern of the artist, to recreate out of the disorder of life that order which is art.*

With frank and plainspoken language, the poet transforms experience into a narrative of becoming—writer, wife, mother—driven by the "harsh resolve to talk back/even if it's nothing more than this,/a romp through a few stanzas." There is a kind of playfulness here, but it is the kind of play, as on the schoolyard with its taunts and cruelties, that brackets the most serious of human interactions.

Early in the collection the poem "Drinking" reveals, with an apt image, the poet's inheritance as the speaker, addressing the self, imagines her father: "So you sit there, angry, watching his head bobbing/to stay upright, like a prisoner whose just been interrogated/and told you everything he knows."

In *Underlife,* O'Neil interrogates and gives voice to personal experience with compelling honesty. Resisting silence, these poems give order to dis-order and tell us everything they aim to know about our beautiful and troubled lives. By the collection's end, we've journeyed with the poet through an intimate terrain, a transformation of life into art.

–Natasha Trethewey

UNDERLIFE

EARLY MEMORY

Nothing Fancy

I am from hush puppies & barbecue
from chitlins & fatbacks
hog maws & hog jaws & grits & scrapple.
Outside stands a dogwood tree we have let
overgrow from laziness
& a driveway cracked
with blades of grass.
I am from Rosemary & Stanley,
the last model in the series.
Around our house honeysuckle blesses the air,
seasons the heat of summer into a main dish.
I am a plum black garnish to the day.
Wafts of smoke from pots on the stove
steam the kitchen.
Salt & Pepper stand at attention
next to the potholders on the counter.
Dinner is ready—no time for parsley.

Old Dog

Sounder! Here girl. Come ...
He shouts to me like I'm a coon dog
chasing possums out in the fields.

The school's back lot became a small country where
names were given but not deserved
and I took it and took it,
even laughed with everyone else
at my own black self, suffering like most of us suffered—

quietly. The laughter so loud you forgot homework,
the blue-and-white uniforms, red veils worn in church,
Jesus on a beaded noose in our pockets.

Today, on this purgatory of a cloudy day,
I stare blankly into an open meadow from my desk
as wind kicks up dust and memory;
more so, the chance to recall
a small morsel of a boy and his big mouth

and my harsh resolve to talk back,
even if it's nothing more than this,
a romp through a few stanzas.
I am grateful for that old dog of memory—
for what it lets you keep
and what it lets you throw away.

Early Memory

I remember picking up a fistful
of sand, smooth crystals, like hourglass sand
and throwing it into the eyes of a boy. Johnny
or Danny or Kevin—*he* was not important.
I was five and I knew he would cry.

I remember everything about it—
the sandbox in the corner of the room
at Cinderella Day Care; Ms. Lee,
who ran over after the boy wailed for his mother,
her stern look as the words *No snack* formed on her lips.
My hands with their gritty, half-mooned fingernails
I hid in the pockets of my blue and white dress.
How she found them and uncurled small sandy fists.

There must have been such rage in me, to give such pain
to another person. This afternoon,
I saw a man pull a gold chain off the neck
of a woman as she crossed the street.
She cried out with a sound that bleached me.
I walked on, unable to help,
knowing that fire in childhood
clenched deep in my pockets all the way home.

Afro Puffs

In kindergarten, I was the only one with Afro puffs.
The only other person at school with a hairstyle even resembling a 'fro
was my dad when he picked me up at the end of the day.
They were stellar long before I knew who Angela Davis was.
My hair was parted down the center into two clusters,
one on each side. Mom used hair grease to oil my scalp
and comb out the naps, with barrettes holding them in place.
Afterward, she used the Afro pick: a short, straight metal comb
with that muscular black plastic hand in salute. To me
it was cold steel that looked like prison bars,
but there was always that fist high above the bars grasping.
We watched *Sanford and Son* and *Good Times*
while fixing my hair, and I knew Willona kept her pick
in her purse. I'd see them sticking out of the back pockets of blue jeans
belonging to the neighborhood kings and queens.
It would be much later before I attached faces to those fists.

Lightning Bugs

What are they made of
that they can frolic and sparkle
above the delicious scent of honeysuckle
on a warm June night?
They'll shine for anyone
to make the world
a little less dull.
And where do they come from?
They glide golden
against the moon's patina,
drifting above
Big Debbie's backyard
and Jr.'s Corner Market.
I sit on the front stoop,
watch then float across well-worn streets,
the blacktop of my misspent youth.
My cupped hands I offer
only to put them in a jar.
They cannot tell me about
captivity or what it means to love
and to set something free.
Still, like a true captor
I detain my bugs until morning
now grateful for release.
To understand malice
I would deny them
the right to shimmer.

Service

The military needed cheap labor
to move office furniture
into the newly remodeled Pentagon,
so they had the grunts do the work.
My father made the 300-mile round-trip
for five weeks to get the job done.
Sometimes he gave rides to other enlisteds,
and charged a small fee to those
who needed a lift.
My father, who in 1969
would have done anything
for his wife and newborn daughter,
put desks together for generals and elite brass
in the oppressive summer heat, in the Summer of Love,
wiping his sweaty face in the mirror
of a bathroom once marked *colored only*
in segregated Virginia.
            One day,
he said, *the higher-ups will realize*
the world is put together by men like me.

Saturn's Child

When my father snores
he sucks in the whole world
and releases it in one pure breath.
At night I'd come into his room
where he would pass out on the bed—
too drunk to change his clothes or
put out his cigarette, which had
burnt itself down to the embers. I would
pull off his shoes and watch him sleep,
smelling his sweet, stale breath
fill the room in waves. He was so tired
I could put my finger into his mouth and pull it out
before he inhaled.
                         Once I let my finger linger a second
too long and his tongue touched the flat of my tip.
I thought of going in deeper, first a hand, then an arm—
the tender cutlet of my body swallowed whole by my
father. But I was barely enough to make him cough.
He rolled over on his side, leaving a well in the space
where his body had been. Crawling back into my own bed,
as my father slept the peaceful sleep of ogres, I felt
the house shake with his rhythmic tremors.

Poem for My Father

Some night just after 10:30,
before mom leaves for the hospital
and you have started her car,
asked if she has money, her mace,
reminded her that she can pull apart
her Club and use its silver shaft as a weapon,
after you have kissed her good-night
and watched her drive off from
the kitchen window as she has for so many nights,
driving over slick downtown streets,
and poured your first Jim Beam,
you think about tomorrow, how it will be just like today:
boring, full of empty talk shows and infomercials,
or consider the possibility of gardening.
Before you walk up the dark stairway to bed,
where you will drink, the TV volume turned low,
it would be nice if you called me, your only daughter,
550 miles from home, paying bills and not sleeping,
as I sit at my keyboard thinking of my father,
who also used to leave about this same time,
pressed and starched in a navy blue uniform,
gold shield, nightstick, bag lunch,
night after night doing a job he hated
and never quit. A fire truck careens around
my street corner and soon
I will turn off my computer and wake
to do the exact same thing tomorrow,
while down south the quiet of your street unnerves you,
so much so you double-lock the front door
and turn on the floodlights,
struck with the memory of how mom once quipped

she wished she could work 16 hours a day instead of eight,
anticipating your need for something to do in retirement
as you stare at a dying lawn and entertain the idea
of feeling the cold brown earth between your fingers,
wondering what has happened to this life you chose.

She's Closest to Breaking

She's closest to breaking
as she hangs over the sink like a broken branch
with just bark and fiber keeping her taut.

She wrenches her hands chaffed raw by dishwashing liquid
and no amount of twisting and soaking
will melt the wedding ring off her finger
or the 35 years out of the band.

It would be so easy to pick up a dish
and smash it against the counter
leaving the pieces for someone else to pick up.

Instead
she washes every last dish
all the while wrenching that finger
under the water.

The Only Time I Ever Saw My Mother Drunk

She bounded into the house with a piece of silver tinsel
wrapped around her neck, tucked inside her coat
like a winter scarf. Dad propped himself up
from door frame to wall to wall.
They had been across the street for hours
visiting our Polynesian neighbors. Mom said
they spent most of the night trying karaoke.
Dad slurred, but was happy to talk about
the neighbors who performed nightly at Blue Hawaii
and their Christmas tree that touched the ceiling.

Suddenly she erupted with a spasm
that bent her body in half. A thick liquid glistened
on the floor. At some point she noticed a contact lens
had fallen out. We knew it was lost
in the chunks on the brown tiled floor.
Mom knelt down, tried to collect the goop with her hands.
Dad just shook his head, started in with *a lawd have mercy,*
then was silent. He watched my mother cry
into her hands, then stumbled out,
knocking over a chair on his way to the bedroom.

Upstairs we heard the rattle of pants and belts
that hung behind the bedroom door. He
fell asleep, made himself unavailable to us
while in the bathroom, I stripped my mother,
wiped the crusty film from her mouth,
and put her to bed in my room.
I held her hand in my two until she
drifted off. While they slept, celery chunks
and cocktail wieners waited for me on the kitchen floor.
Somewhere a lens floated in heavy syrup.

Drinking

A coworker says,
We're thinking about doing a happy hour.
Wanna join us?
And you recall the night you found your father
slumped over in the kitchen chair
after one shot and one beer too many,
the cigarette between his fingers
burning itself into one long ash.
But you go anyway because
it's Friday and your job sucks,
and drinking invites camaraderie.
Besides, deep down you know you love this—
the two-for-one specials for drinks called
woo woos, kamikazes, blow jobs;
the bland bar food and the jukebox
blaring "Proud Mary" over the crowd.
And while you have a break between rounds
you think you see your father sitting there asleep in the dark
with the bare bulb of the porch light
casting shadows on the pots and pans.
At this point, taking off your bra and dancing on
a table seems reasonable. Asking the bartender
to come home with you is not so far-fetched.
And while you couldn't possibly finish
the last cold fried cheese stick on the plate
you think of leaving but where would you go?
You are no longer attached to this world.
Putting the key into the ignition becomes a real task.
So you sit there, angry, watching his head bobbing
to stay upright, like a prisoner who has just been interrogated
and told you everything he knows.

Permanent

Dipping my head under the hot-cold water
of the kitchen sink
I feel her hand, her wedding ring lightly rubbing my head
slowly, not to cause burning, yet my scalp starts to feel
like angry ants stamping formation.
Afternoon whittles itself into evening
as my mother opens the window to
the bruise-colored sky.
We open to a moment of permanent,
neutralizing shampoo, and perm strengthener.
This is my last night home.
I am learning how to do this,
the opening and closing of her fingers on top of my
fingers shampooing,
our hands turning into prunes
She tells me to be careful in my new life,
she says, *the ones in your generation are always burning.*
Rinse, towel off
her hands are on my head.
If there is too much air close the window.
Rinse again.
Rinse.

Night Work

After the families have visited for the evening, tethered their well wishes like
balloons to the backs of chairs, taken photos of the first hours of life, my mother
checks in on the preemies, often healthy but occasionally too yellow, or pink, or blue.
Deflated and in need of oxygen, they are held together by some order,
exhausted by the urgency of being saved. For every tiny
fledgling that leaves the unit, there is always another in need of touch.
Gloved, my mother cared through a thin layer of separation while
holding the head of a baby born smaller than a shadow.
I think she liked the all-nighters, especially in early
January, babies born just after the New Year. She liked doing the
kind things that love cannot do: adjusting another woman's breast,
lifting the pillow under her head so the baby slips just above the
mother's ribs, offering advice or comfort before returning to the
NICU, the tectonic plates of mother and child drifting together then apart.
Often she delighted in the midnight coos, a love song for the
phantom ache of babies she could never carry, those tiny loaves
quick, unleavened, so eager to take touch like communion, while she loved what
remained, leaving her impoverished soul open and gaping.
She shuffled through our house as if it had long, antiseptic corridors,
there but not there. Such is the life of one in service to others,
under no illusions about the gift of grace. My mother, whose
voice is the sound of love becoming, seldom wondered
what became of those raindrops, whose first days of life were
X-rayed, poked, prodded—their sentences commuted to time served.
Yet, they will not remember this time when they were barely more than
zygotes, as it should be. As if they were never there.

Self-Portrait

This face that I love
given to me by Stanley and Rosemary
is laminated to the blue background
of my driver's license.
The Prince William County seal opens like a sunflower.
I will be 120 lbs until the year 20XX.

A TRUE STORY

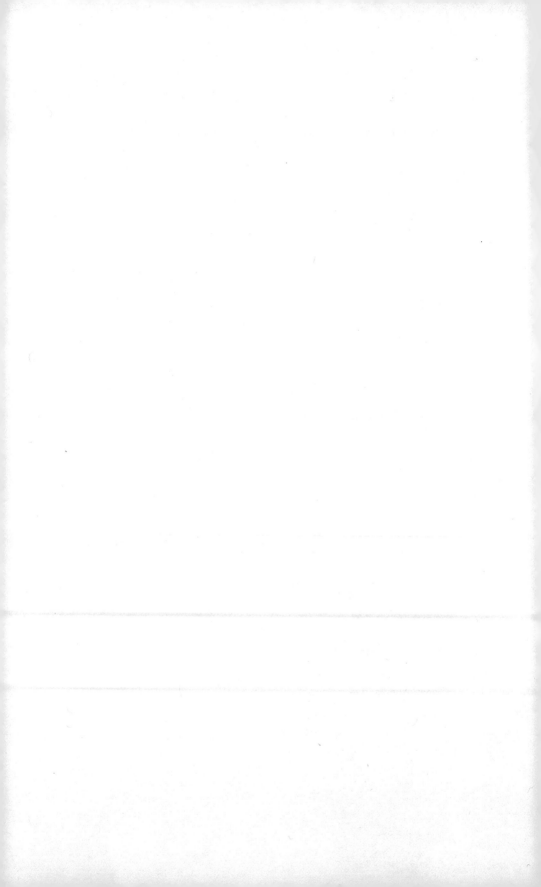

How to Make a Crab Cake

Start with your own body,
the small bones of the hands
moving toward the inlets of the fingers.

Wanting it too much invites haste.
You must love what is raw
and hungered for.

Think of the crab cake as the ending,
as you till away at the meat, digging for
errant shells and jagged edges.

Always, it's a matter of guesswork
but you hold it together
by the simplest of ingredients,

for this is how the body learns to be generous,
to forgive the flaws inherited
and enjoy what lies ahead.

Yet you never quite know
when it happens,
the moment when the lumps

transcend egg and breadcrumbs,
the quiver of oil in a hot pan,
to become unworldly:

the manifold of pleasure
with the sweet ache of crab
still bright on your tongue.

In Praise of Okra

No one believes in you
like I do. I sit you down on the table
& they overlook you for
fried chicken & grits,
crab cakes & hush puppies,
black-eyed peas & succotash
& sweet potatoes & watermelon.

Your stringy, slippery texture
reminds them of the creature
from the movie *Aliens*.

But I tell my friends if they don't like you
they are cheating themselves;
you were brought from Africa
as seeds, hidden in the ears and hair
of slaves.

Nothing was wasted in our kitchens.
We took the unused & the throwaways
& made feasts;
we taught our children
how to survive,
adapt.

So I write this poem
in praise of okra
& the cooks who understood
how to make something out of nothing.
Your fibrous skin
melts in my mouth—

green flecks of flavor,
still tough, unbruised,
part of the fabric of earth.
Soul food.

A True Story

Once a friend in Arizona
bought a cactus plant,
heart shaped, with a yellow bud
tilted elegantly to the side

like a woman's good Sunday hat.
She placed the gray clay pot
on her coffee table,
and after a few days she noticed

that the plant started to move.
Concerned, she called a flower shop,
asking the florist,
How can I get it to stop?

The florist shrieked, *Get out of
the house!* He called the police,
the fire department, a pet store—
A man in a beekeeper's garb

(all the town could afford),
roped off the house and the yard,
placed the plant in the middle of the lawn,
and split it wide open like a watermelon

to find a nest of scorpions writhing
in the afternoon sun.
Displaced, motherless,
those hothouse babies,

hidden under the cactus' tough, sharp spines,
waved their feelers,
bowed their heads,
as if they were guilty of something.

The Young Girl

Wandering through the aisles of the department store,
a security guard notices her
lingering among the racks of costume jewelry.
He thinks he saw a young black girl stuff something
into her bag. The guard stops her at the double doors
and searches the backpack. Nothing is found,
nothing is explained, yet he looks at her as if
he has seen her face before. She shuffles her feet as
the manager's name is called over the loud speaker.
The guard squawks into his walkie-talkie:
She fits the description.

Fumbling through my purse, I wonder about her
thin brown body; how many times has she been
stopped, opened up in the front of drug stores
and clothing stores. How many times
have buzzers sounded and heavy eyes
fallen on her face.

The manager threatens to call the police.
Her big gold-hooped earrings dangle
under a brown baseball cap, hiding her eyes
from the customers in line.
The lady behind me says,
She's gonna cry. For a moment
the young girl glances up, looks at me,
then looks away. She turns toward the guard
and starts smacking her gum loudly—
a series of rapid pops like a cap gun.
I crack a slight smile. I hope she took it!

X's and O's

At the cocktail party
you are the X
in a room full of O's.
They are everywhere
while you, the lone X,
wait in silence
for your first engagement
into conversation
that never comes.
How they think you don't notice:
crossing the room
to avoid conversation,
pretending, if approached,
not to hear,
going out of their way
to deny acquaintance.
The X is used to going it alone.
From their vantage
displeasure is X.
And there you are
in medias res—
every insecurity
filling your pockets
like old napkins.
What do you really know
of this world
and its soft hurts?
What do you know about
the power of X? Still,
you have to give it to the O's—

they recognize the order of things,
and how to speak the words
not to be spoken.

At the Subway

As she stumbles through the subway car,
her laughter cracks open the seal on the day.
Her eyes are glassy and pink like a fish
on an ice bed. She cackles for no apparent reason,
perhaps at some joke funny only to her.
Newspapers rise and heads burrow into books as she passes.
I try not to look
but feel her plum black skin and soiled jeans
coming toward me.
She takes off her sweatshirt and drops it
on my feet. I kick it away.
The woman looks to me as if to say,
pick it up.
This woman, this joker that fell out of the playing deck,
wants to open me up and scoop me out,
but I feel myself turning hard, into bark;
shaking the leaves off my branches, knuckling my toes
into the floor like roots.
I wait. She waits.
A muffled voice announces the next stop over the loud speaker.
The woman picks up the sweatshirt, tucks the bundle
under her arm, and moves onto the platform.
I sit there, waiting for the sap
to run back into my body.
Her laugh rides with me on the train.
I hear the dry crackle of leaves being crushed underfoot.

Drone

Here we are now, the wasp trapped between the window and me.
He feels the cool breeze of freedom like a secret lament.
This is the last time I'll see him alive. But he's moving on
and so am I. Today I am speaking in the mother tongue
in which living and dying is the same language. Today
I want to hurt something, smash something between glass and hand.
The wasp in his black muscle T and striped pants so tight
his ass looks like a bubble. I tap the pane. Watch his antennae move.
He must feel grounded. Or cornered. Misses his mother.
God Save the Queen. God's mercy is missing.
Maybe he's lost hope. Maybe he wants to jump.
Or wait for the wasp rescue squad that's just not coming.
And after his passing, I'll speak fondly of him
as if he never made the wrong choices. Never climbed
around my neck to sting me. I will never forget the redness,
the swelling—the gift that keeps on giving.
But you must move on and so must I. Does he believe in posterity?
Decorum implies that I stop but retaliation seems the only way.
I am the horrifying other who can't be located or identified. I am
God's missing mercy. Today we'll gather our incomplete information,
our faint knowledge of each other, and plot each other's destruction.
He cannot find his way back to the cool breeze of freedom.
This is the last time he'll see me alive. Today I struggled. He struggled.
The universal *you* struggled. Without sentiment. It happened.
Here we are now.

True Story #2: Missing

First a foot, then the whole body
found wedged upside down behind
a tall bookcase,

a young woman missing in a home
she shared with her family
most of her life.

Eleven days misplaced,
the police surmised she simply fell
adjusting a TV plug behind the shelves—

simply, as if she disappeared
to that land of lost socks and
missing keys

and could be retrieved
simply by believing it so.
Her sister passed her bedroom

without stopping to look
but could not put her finger
on that unfamiliar odor

soaking the house in loss.
It doesn't matter, at this point,
if they believed it was a kidnapping,

or death or escape.
Only the following remains:
a little thing miscalculated, collapsed,

and gave way. What new fear
will guide their silent house at night—
her absence pinned against a plaster wall.

In the end, it wasn't enough
to see her every day,
to love her silence and her shaky grace.

They seem convinced of
a quiet so deep
even common sense can't intrude on it.

Poem About Nuts

Dear sweet scrota. You have suffered in my jokes
and for that I am sorry. Little nut bags, I have subjected you
to quips about shrinkage and rhymes about size. Those colorful nicknames
you have in the modern vernacular—kibbles & bits, bangers & mash,
red bliss potatoes—always make me smile. How rude of me!
You serve a purpose, which is more than I can say for the appendix,
the avocado, and the giraffe. You are servants to your master,
who doesn't always think with his head. And that joke I made
about the boys on their way to see the pope … my apologies.
That was just wrong.

Sex and Pizza

Once a classmate told me
Sex is like pizza:
no matter how bad it is,
it's still pizza. Strange, coming
from one of the unsexiest people
I knew. Didn't believe him
until my early 20s
when all I wanted was hard,
kinked-out, unexplainable sex.
9 ½ Weeks sex. *Blue Velvet* sex.
The small town of my body
sent me outward to a friend
as local as my fingertips.
His body, beautifully taut,
and I was happy hour
poured into a miniskirt.
Before we knew it,
the quick blows of our bodies
struck together like rocks
catching spark.
Ass up, head down,
no stroking, no kissing,
just clumsy, fractional fucking
that was over before it began.
I remember walking
into the unfamiliar daylight,
sleep deprived and scorched
like a house gutted by fire.
Years later, I think
my classmate was right.
How else can I explain

the lip-biting, sloppy goodness
of exploration, of bodies seeking
those fine mistakes and digressions,
the cock and the pussy,
the world dividing into hemispheres,
sliced into its imperfect selves.

THE RIPE TIME

Morning Poem

An hour before sunrise,
I put on my red robe
and walk the dark halls of the house,
listening to its creaking under my feet.
I look into the bathroom mirror,
see the oval of my mother's face,
warm chestnut. She reminds me
to wipe the sleep out of my eyes,
to smooth lotion on my skin,
keeping it soft and ageless.
Not a laugh line or crow's foot to be found.
I ask her how this poem should end.

Something I Needed

Dig deep, my husband says.
I look to him as subject because
I am empty. So I reach back to when

the writing came easy, when poems
fell like tree branches in a storm
and it was always raining.

Young and single, we started
when he asked me to dance,
spinning on F&M's pool table,

all hind legs and haunches until 4 a.m.
We ate alligator nuggets and Crawfish Monica
in the jazz of a crescent city.

Now he dares me to make our suburbia poetic.
Yet I long for a time without prudence,
biting into beignets at the Café Du Monde.

Even as my son rejects the peanut butter sandwich
I stop writing the poem to make,
I am flummoxed,

as if I couldn't put my mind on something I needed,
so that everything I imagined to say
might be tethered to this rough tongue forever.

Sugar

I pour a tablespoon of sugar on my kitchen counter,
spreading it thin with the back of my spoon.
Each grain becomes a moment,
a seed resting on tilled earth,
the words forming in my husband's mouth as he says
kiss me, and I am reminded again and again
of the first, the beginning, the newness of his mouth,
his plump lips deciphering the arc
of my teeth; his tongue a new species born
in my vast ocean. I myself a creature,
made of sugar and water,
capable of dissolving right out of existence,
salvation and destruction in one sweet instant.
Each granule is a lost poem, an unanswerable wish
spinning on the edge of consciousness.
I say to the pots and pans: every human narrative
requires an act of nature.
I tell my story to the cereal boxes, the soup cans—
they turn their labels away in disbelief;
their stupefied lids open wide like paper sacks.
For every truth I hold to be self-evident,
I touch the flat of my tongue
to the counter's surface.

Tuesday

The dark laurel of rain over our heads
means that everyone's under the weather today.
June in New England, the sky aching
from rain so hard and unexpected
the weatherman sends his apologies.

I slink into the house, sopping wet.
My husband and I kiss as if
I've just come home from shore leave.
I've come home wanting to touch
and be touched, so much wetness

outside. Sometimes I am drawn into child's play
and dinner and the clothes to protect me
tomorrow, but tonight I uncork the wine,
allow myself to want what the body wants
as the humidity beads and slowly
rolls down the windowpane.

I touch the small of his back
and let my hand glide lower
while he slices red peppers for salad.
Tonight, let's be careless and sloppy
like drivers testing the speed limit,
not watching the ponding in the road.

Rough Country

Sweet Baby, I have imagined your death
since the day we met: a horrific tragedy
that begins with me getting *the call.*
You're the victim: the devil's plaything
sandwiched between the cabs
of two tractor trailers, fodder for rubberneckers
and a story for the evening news;
or a slip of the chainsaw while sawing wood;
or worse, an escaped convict finds the chainsaw
making you victim #1 in his blood thirst.
Or maybe it's something simpler: salmonella,
falling through a sidewalk grate,
walking pneumonia (my personal favorite),
a piano falling from the sky. And always
I am locked away in a moment of numbness
like smashing my thumb with a hammer,
the perpetual hurt that pains to the core.
So as our children sleep unaware in their room,
as I touch your strong, worn face,
kiss those lips that taste like rain-soaked nights,
my senses begin again to commit you to memory,
only to be reborn, back into the same rough country
weighing inside my brain like an anvil.

The Ripe Time

Each month she thinks her nipples
are becoming more tender,
areolas blooming into wild ginger.
Before her is a bed filled with ardor.

Pregnant, not pregnant,
she is the princess without the pea—
a ball stuck in the pinball machine
that tilts like clockwork.

After making love
they lie on their sides silvered with sweat.
She listens for the soft chirp of her own breathing:
it does not reveal why her body operates
like a failed business.

On this night
where marriage is the only safe place
she can go, her husband holds her,
tells her it's just a matter of time.

But all she can think about
is this empty house they can't afford
and the ripe tomatoes growing in backyard containers,
smooth-fleshed and heavy,
falling from their stems.

The Fly

Has it been there the whole time? you ask. Curious spectator,
trapped in the bombed-out crash site of my room. Silent. Kinetic.
Only an hour ago I was staring up at you, nostrils flaring, thrusting
deep within my thickets of pubic hair, a thousand coiled snakes
guarding my stamen, my *Jack in the Pulpit.* We lie among candlewicks,
burned into black nubs; sheets filled with moons and stars,
balled up in the right corner of my bed. The wet tangy smell
of sex and sweat hangs over this lost weekend, the weekend our
instinct kicked in. This weekend we became carnivores, going
to that place, that wildlife refuge where the most feared, protected
animals roam; where the mattress shakes and bangs into the walls,
the bed springs coil and recoil from the weight of pleasure. Tonight
we slip and slide and pull the room into us, taking the chairs,
the table, the bed, the paint off the walls, leaving here nothing,
nothing but this.

Not What You Expected

Snow—38 inches,
jackpot! Everywhere there's white
pine trees crusted over,
houses frozen brittle, and
everyone's bone-weary.
At first it's nothing, a flake
melting on your naked arm, and then another
bringing with it the most present absence.
Your great story started with so much promise:
the southerner stuck in New England,
the money not saved, the children you can't carry,
the ice dam on the roof—is that a metaphor for life?
Your windshield wipers are dying.
Misery is the sound of snow and,
dear God, what could happen next?
You're pregnant again and it's your father,
he's having heart palpitations—he's going in
for some tests. Fucking February. If you think you're at a crossroads,
you are. So much snow but is that a purple crocus—
a flash of genius—sprouting smack-dab through the muddy slush?

Always, There's Something

Every house hides a story—
ask it about the grout,
the knots in the hardwood floor,
the dirty secrets we share
between the sink and the sponge.

Days press down on me
like an iron on a silk blouse.

First there are the insufficient wants:
stockpiles of clothes and toys,
movie ticket stubs from 1986,
pictures of people I loved once.

And then there is this need
to ask for help, to be impoverished.
I talk to the closet, tell the clothes
my story—they send their regrets,
say, *Don't dust anything taller*
than your tallest friend.

Always there's something
wanting to be something else.
A glass cake dome
becomes a tabletop garden
—a hothouse for baby tears
is a blessed moment of escape.

What the House Might Say

The Hardwood Floor
My boards ache.
I've lost my luster.
I used to be inspired by
the small earth under me,
but you can walk over me
only so many times before
I turn my planks against you.

The Area Rug
Since I moved to the spare bedroom
I long for your stiff pine
against my back.
Your every flaw
creates memories
I hold deep within my fibers.
I miss protecting you.

The Stove
My eyes are crusty, always covered
with the butt of a pan. Once
I was the hot shot around here.
Now the microwave and I
share a difficult companionship.
No one fries anymore.
Why am I here?

The Microwave
Some days,
I'm just not fast enough.
10 seconds, 20 seconds, half-hour—

trying to beat my own best time.
Someone's always watching me,
but I'm more than a flash in the pan.

Touch my buttons again and
I'll break your fingers.

The Fan
Can you hear me?
I whisper your name back and forth
across a balmy room.
Dust me.
I need to be cleaned.
I shake my head in disapproval,
reveal my slow-turning
pain.

The Telephone
Stop calling me.

The Bathtub
When I feel empty,
I pretend I am a pool,
or an ocean
so vast there is no floor
and no end in sight.
When all else fails
I am the last resort,
the only place left to go.

The Crib
I hear everything:
soft sighs
tucked between

the folds of the sheets.
The mattress imprint
leaves the impression
of a life being lived.

THE UNDERLIFE

Poem for My Infant Son

That first night,
I made your father
sleep with the lights on
so I could make sure
you were still breathing.
Your brown body so malleable
one false move could
break you forever.
You are all feet and inches,
cooing a song I've never heard
in a language I don't understand.
Yet you have taught us in your own way,
loved us even when we
try, fail, fail again.
That's what children do.

Baby boy,
my lamb,
my suckling,
my colt,
you look at me like
I am your whole world
but the truth is
you are mine.

The Small Plans

You won't remember this.
Not the shallow breathing and gray lips.
Not the vomit. Not the milk
that overtook you like a breached levee.
Remember nothing.
Not your heart.
Your heart.
A hymn beating so faintly.
Not the midnight emergency visit or the staff
of 15 swelling to save your little life.
Not the incision, your line of demarcation.
Not your muscles working against each other,
despite each other.
Forget coarctation.
Forget the tubes, the IVs,
the doctors with their bad jokes,
the nurses with their latexed hands.
Not your father feeding you sugar water
with a cotton swab, or your mother
kissing your lips pursed tight as a clasp,
those perfect lips God gave you.
Is it true He doesn't give you more than you can bear?
Forget I asked.
Forget Him.
Forget the small plans we have for today,
watching you vanish and reappear
in the space of my hands.
You, who have been blessed by pain,
forget your first two weeks of life.
Amen.

Ella

1.

Queen of the queen-sized bed,
she sleeps between us,
arms outstretched like a plus sign,

Then she rolls to her side,
back facing her true north father,
her fat foot buttressing my jiggly belly.

Somehow she latches onto sleep, never fearing
that I could crush the life right out of her
with the body that gave it.

No—her snoring is a mother's aria
filling the room
with her sweet music.

2.

Round midnight
she's gumming for me,
nudging for a swig of warm milk.

I let down and she takes me in,
cupping her hands around
my milk-full breast.

And when she falls asleep,
crazy drunk, I pull away—
she continues to suck

as if I am still there.
The next morning,
her jagged little teeth rub me awake.

Under my blouse
my sore, cracked nipple
is a jewel of pain.

Tangerines

Seems like yesterday you were in my dream
Formed inside my body as a pearl
Last night I nibbled your feet like tangerines

Those plump sections, with meaty toes in between
Pebbly skin, your thin rind a dizzying whirl
Seems like yesterday you were in my dream

Your hand holds tight to a crumbled saltine,
What you cherish most, I try to unfurl
Last night I nibbled your feet like tangerines

I think about your soft fruit, still pristine,
Before your hair tilts up in a sexy curl
Seems like yesterday you were in my dream

I'll wake up from this and replay the scene,
The moment you say your life is yours, let it unfurl
Last night I nibbled your feet like tangerines

You'll grow up, grow older, my little bean
To tell me you just can't help being a girl
Seems like yesterday you were in my dream
Last night I nibbled your feet like tangerines

The Kerning

Today I spent the morning
brushing pink crayon
from your teeth. This tells me
you know how to eat words.
You've tasted those intangible calories
that fill my cavernous heart.
You're beginning to understand
how sloppy and brutal the imagination can be.
I put my hands between your pearly teeth
and yank petals of paper from your mouth.
Someday I will teach you how to read
words that are not there,
show you how to breathe without
disturbing the air. Nothing lives
outside of us in this overprinted world.
Decide for yourself. Then let me know
if you can eat a crayon without leaving
a mark.

What Mommy Wants
—*after Kim Addonizio*

I want a pair of Candie's.
Make them cheap and tacky.
High-heeled wooden stilettos
(*stiletto,* from the Italian word for "dagger"),
white leather upper with silver studs along the sides.
Open-toed pumps, with just enough wiggle room
for my toes painted *No, I'm Not a Waitress* red.
I want a pair of Candie's.
Make my legs curvy and dangerous.
I want to strut down the street
in a pair of Daisy Dukes and a halter top
past O'Buster's fruit stand,
past Coffee Time donut shop with its real cream bismarcks
and apple cider crullers, past the wobbly scaffolding
and morning commuters at the train station.
I want the hard hats on break
to drop their coffees and shout,
Nice gams!
I want women to take one look at me and think
Here comes trouble.
I want to be a tawdry wench,
the kind of woman mothers warn their sons about,
the kind that makes a priest give up religion.
I want my husband to strip me naked
bend me over
leaving on just my Candie's
as if he were cheating on his wife
and getting away with it.

Discipline

The next time it acts up
Hit it with a rolled-up newspaper
Hit it because it wants something
Hit it until it goes away
Because it makes that incessant racket
Because it wants your attention
Because it cries
Hit it because you are annoyed beyond annoyance
Because talking is not enough
Hit it with last Sunday's sports section
Rolled up like a nightstick
Or a Louisville Slugger
Hit it with the back of your hand
Hit it with the flat of your palm
Pop it in the mouth
On the head
On the ears so they ring
Hit it on the small of the back
Hit it again and again and again
Make it stop
Make sure it won't do it again
Make it understand
Because it never learns a lesson
Once is not enough
Once more, for good measure
Knock the shit out of it
Knock some sense into it
Knock it into the middle of next week
Because it asked for it
Hit it because you feed it
You keep it warm

You give it a place to sleep
And still it won't listen
Hit it because it loves you no matter what
Hit it because you can

Cow Logic

They are dumb,
I think.
All those years behind
gates and stalls,
Eating silage.
Getting milked.
Females
listening to the voices
of feeders and milkers,
recovering phrases
the way mothers
overhear conversations
that rise from the backseat of the car.
What do cows do? my son asks.
They live out there in the green fields.
All they have to do is eat grass
and moo all day
and take care of their babies,
I say.
And maybe that's all
kids in backseats
need to know
about what we do—
we make milk
we have babies
we stand up a lot
we give ice cream
and look at the big sky
all day.

Back from Maternity Leave
—*after John Updike*

"Did anyone miss me?" the new mommy asks,
amazed to find the working world just as she left it.

Her absence not even a crack in the
glass ceiling sky. Clients failed to notice her return,

promotions were handed out like candy, and
time flowed through their hands like paper clips.

The desk jockeys think she's moonlighting when
she describes the first toothless smile, the first giggle,

the first time her daughter holds her finger
while feeding from her swollen breasts.

Just a pile of new project files marks her return.
Her office door closes in lockdown.

The cosmic tumblers click shut.
The yoke still fits, warm as if never unbridled.

The Editor Speaks

There is flow among the elements
on a page. Word buttressing word,
lines asleep on a featherbed of 80-pound stock.
After all, the newsletter you're reading
is an ecosystem for language,
and there you are preening and sorting
someone else's natural selection. Your hands part
the cool water of the page's surface,
splashing letters in your face—
every voluptuous character, every minuscule glyph
rolling down your cheek as beautiful as tears.
Yet all that negative space bends to
the wind's slightest rustle,
keeping the kerning in sync with the leading,
the tracking aligned with meaning.
Everything gives off a vibration—
just listen to the callout box and what it calls:
Helvetica opens its beak to Galliard,
while the serifs bloom their impossible hues.
They fling themselves against the synapses of the brain,
until something frilled and pithy is born,
something elemental but not original.
The trick is not to care about any of that.
You hold your red pen like a torch
as you run through a forest of thickly settled text
only looking back to see what branches
you have burned.

For Terence

When a man dies,
you must lay your ear
to his chest, hear the
non-beating of his heart,
be drawn in by the silence
that bonds you to this moment.
Even if you have nothing to say,
even if you do not know the deceased,
even if you never loved each other,
lean in close. Closer.
Lower yourself into the casket.
Slip your hand under his shirt.
The last touch of this world
is bare.

Saying Yes

If you find yourself awake
and alone at 4:30 in the morning,
you wait until you hear
that first bump against the wall,
the shifting of sheets,
the bounce of bed springs.
You wait for the first toy
to be kicked and some obnoxiously
loud children's song to disturb the air,
and the shuffle of footed pajamas
on hardwood floor to follow.
You've waited for this moment
all night, maybe all your life,
when that ghostly half figure
enters your darkened room,
nothing visible but his outline.
Before your box of a voice
finds its first words of the day,
you wait until your son
tugs on your arm and says, *Mommy?*
All you have to do is say
Yes.

Contrition

My son asks me how to write a poem
I tell him the story about the woman
who feeds her son oatmeal. He doesn't want it
but she doesn't see that—or maybe she does,
jamming the spoon into his clenched mouth
until she hears it clang against his
chipped teeth. He cries, says he's sorry.
She puts him in time-out where
he sits facing the wall for hours,
days, years, threatens to throw him
into the middle of next week if he turns around.
He sits there until he faces her as a man. She asks,
Do you remember the color of the oatmeal bowl?
Now you're ready to write a poem.

Time Map

Which letter to write
Which book to read
Which room in the house to clean
and how deeply
Which window to open to allow in the most breeze
Which cloud, which curve of the air
Which lawns have the most dandelions punctuating the grass
like ellipses, what gets said, what's left out
Which lawns, besides ours, have no nutritional value
Which forsythia branches to clip
Which sticks to bundle for rubbish
Which ones to adorn the living room mantle
next to the wedding photo,
the crystal egg, the clock with its incessant ticking
Which neighbor will drop by with our misdelivered mail
Which neighbors won't say hi when I stand in the front yard,
with their small lots and big fat driveways
Which ones think my grass is greener
Which Cheetos to eat as my son counts them in the bag
with his cheesy little fingers
Which happiness, too many to choose

Take Care
—for TPO

I like those words much more than
sincerely, best, or cheers—
words that have become trite
yet expected at the end of a card
or a thank-you note, losing their meaning
when out of context. Tell someone to take care
and you've given a directive.
Be careful.
Protect your strange and beautiful
underlife. Protect yourself from
the boundless nimbus:
what mothers fear a child will find
once he leaves the oval of her arms.
A wish for you, love, to move against
the abstract, ever-present danger
that calls all things to an end
like a letter, or a poem.

January   Gill O'Neal

ACKNOWLEDGMENTS

The following poems first appeared in the following publications or Web sites. Many thanks to them all.

Babel Fruit.com: "Contrition," "Drone," "True Story #2: Missing"
Can We Have Our Ball Back.com: "Discipline," "Afro Puffs," "The Fly"
Callaloo: "The Young Girl"
Cave Canem II Anthology: "Saturn's Child"
Crab Creek Review: "The Kerning"
Drunken Boat: "The Editor Speaks"
Field: "Drinking"
Edible Phoenix: "In Praise of Okra"
Literal Latte: "Nothing Fancy" (formerly "Where I Come From")
Literary Mama.com: "The Ripe Time"
Ouroboros Review: "Old Dog"
Stuff Magazine: "Early Memory"

"Night Work" won the 2007 Eagle Tribune/Robert Frost Poetry Foundation Spring Poetry Contest. It was published by the Eagle Tribune Newspapers.

A debt I can never repay. My heartfelt thanks to my teachers: Toi Derricotte, Sharon Olds, Philip Levine, Galway Kinnell, and Ruth Stone.

To Joseph Legaspi, "I loves me some Jo Jo!"

Thank you to Cave Canem (CC!), Erin Dionne, Alex Sembra, Kristi Bernstein, Suzie McGlone, Tim O'Neil, Christine Junge, Eric Stich, Maureen Lederhos, Babson College Marketing (Pubs!), Mary O'Donoghue, Natasha Trethewey, Baron Wormser, Jim Brock, Afaa Michael Weaver, Denise Duhamel, Poetry Thursday.com, Read Write Poem.com, The Robert Frost Foundation, The Salem Writers' Group, and the community of poets and writers in the blogosphere.

Special thanks to all my family and friends, near and far, always close to my heart.

OTHER BOOKS IN THE NEW VOICES SERIES

A Day This Lit, Howard Levey
Kazimierz Square, Karen Chase
So Close, Peggy Penn
Silk Elegy, Sandra Gash
Palace of Ashes, Sherry Fairchok
Life with Sam, Elizabeth Hutner
GlOrious, Joan Cusack Handler
Rattle, Eloise Bruce
Soft Box, Celia Brand
Momentum, Catherine Doty
Imperfect Lover, Georgianna Orsini
Eye Level, 50 Histories, Christopher Matthews
Body of Diminishing Motion, Joan Seliger Sidney
The Singers I Prefer, Christian Barter
The Fork Without Hunger, Laurie Lamon
To the Marrow, Robert Seder
The Disheveled Bed, Andrea Carter Brown
The Silence of Men, Richard Jeffrey Newman
Against Which, Ross Gay
Through a Gate of Trees, Susan Jackson
Imago, Joseph O. Legaspi
We Aren't Who We Are and this world isn't either, Christine Korfhage
Elegy for the Floater, Teresa Carson
The Second Night of the Spirit, Bhisham Bherwani

CAVANKERRY'S MISSION

Through publishing and programming, CavanKerry Press
connects communities of writers with communities of readers.
We publish poetry that reaches from the page to include the
reader, by the finest new and established contemporary writers.
Our programming brings our books and our poets to
people where they live, cultivating new audiences
and nourishing established ones.

CavanKerry now uses only recycled paper in its book production.

Printing this book on 30% PCW and
FSC certified paper saved 2 trees,

1 million BTUs of energy, 127lbs. of CO_2,

67lbs. of solid waste, and 524 gallons of water.